UNLEASH YOUR
NATURAL TALENT

UNLEASH YOUR NATURAL TALENT

A Logical Pathway to Sports Success

Eugene Joseph McConnin

Library of Congress Control Number:		2019910190
ISBN:	Hardcover	978-1-7960-0503-5
	Softcover	978-1-7960-0502-8
	eBook	978-1-7960-0501-1

Print information available on the last page.

Rev. date: 08/16/2019

To order additional copies of this book, contact:
Xlibris
1-800-455-039
www.Xlibris.com.au
Orders@Xlibris.com.au
793278

PREFACE

Some of the information in this book has evolved over the course of my treatment of sports injuries (over forty years) at my chiropractic clinics in Perth, Western Australia, and Buffalo, New York, USA. However, most of it draws on practical and specific application of the natural laws and principles that govern our species. As the observations are logical—and what is logical is right—they have the potential to eventually lead to a revolution in sports training, giving those who are perceptive enough to accept and employ them the edge over their competitors until such programmes are universally embraced. There is nothing theoretical about this approach; it relies on fact. And an overarching fact is that a theory is something that remains unproven.

Eugene McConnin

ACKNOWLEDGEMENTS

In memory of Eugene Joseph McConnin, DC (1930–2016). As promised, I have kept my word in bringing your first manuscript to realisation.

Your many light-bulb moments and nudges day and night; your constant rehashing of concepts over and over again; your joyful, seemingly odd, posturing to reconstruct movement and alignment, often when out and about, have been part of an exceptional mission. The forensic analysis of your multitude of early sporting endeavours to get it all right and your passionate, humorous, quirky, enlightened conversations along the way have led to a single purpose: to share your vision, for the love of all people, that education and sport go hand in hand and open up great opportunities in life.

We put an advertisement in *The West Australian* newspaper nearly thirty years ago, and Greg Smith (Smithy) was one of the standout cartoonists we talked to. His regular Saturday afternoon sessions stimulated Eugene's visions to help create outstanding illustrations from Smithy's imaginative gift. Now known worldwide, Smithy has also updated his illustrations to reflect today's significant credible values.

Highly recommended by Smithy, editor Gary McGay's invaluable, soulful insight and worldly experience in major newspapers and book editing have guided this project through the multitude of intricacies (or idiosyncrasies) the publishing world has thrown at this inexperienced older toddler (me). A dear thank you to him.

Then there are my proofreaders, Marie Czajka and her son, Michael Czajka. Their dedicated energy kept Eugene's fire burning. My great friend Marie, your steadfast, calm influence has helped me in the many challenges life has presented over the years. Michael, your meticulous, focused proofreading abilities proved so valuable, adding another feather to your already many-feathered cap.

Our first typist Julie's great expertise in the initial set-up of many of Eugene's projects deserves special thanks. She is such a wonderful lady. She is devoted to her family and is a multiskilled secretary and popular Dutch radio announcer.

Our second typist Linda's enthusiastic, gentle nature and talent were highly valued in continuing the enlightening work of Eugene's manuscripts. Her presence was much appreciated.

To everyone associated with the publishing of Eugene Joseph McConnin's first book, Unleash Your Natural Talent, we deeply thank you for all your time and effort.

Yours sincerely,
Vicki L. Webster

INTRODUCTION

This book is not just another collection, anthology, or manual of useful tips, insights, techniques, or other information on how to improve one's sports performance, by some famous athlete who may be too old to play any more but not too old to try to regain some lost glory through trying to exploit his popularity. That said, the intention is not to imply that all such advice is totally worthless, but to emphasise the uniqueness of this book.

It is not just another individual's personal interpretation but the revelation of the exact scientific laws governing sports training or the development of sports skills—or any skill for that matter. In time, these irrefutable principles will be adopted by everyone who is serious about training.

In the meantime, or until such time as the acceptance of such methodology is widespread and the general standards are raised accordingly, those who now embrace them will enjoy considerable leverage over the less well-informed or the short-sighted competitors who fail to do so.

Traditionally, all previous information on technique, whether oral or written, has been designed to help you reach your potential. The information in this book will show you how to expand that potential by developing natural talent to exceed conventional expectations.

It seems most people believe that potential is determined during the sensitive early years of childhood, which is undeniably a time during which we absorb information spontaneously. While this facility does pass with that early period of development, progress can still be prodigious—even if it can no longer be spontaneous—when the methodology or approach is correct. Since it has not been, it has misled us into wrongly assuming that any prodigious rate of learning must also be confined to that fleeting early period of spontaneity.

Not understanding the essential difference between the amateur and the professional player, we chose to conceal our ignorance behind the label of natural talent. This is not to imply that such a phenomenon does not exist; it only points out that it is being used—even exploited—to conceal our ignorance.

Many of those who are said to possess natural talent happen to have indulged at some time early in their lives in an often unrelated activity which fortuitously happens to be an ideal preparation for their later skill.

Science tells us that if a certain activity is repeatedly indulged in during what has been identified as the 'sensitive period', the development of the skill involved will be rapid or exponential. Since we are not aware of every activity an individual may have indulged in over the course of his or her life, how can we be certain that some talent is not the result of conditioning rather than genetic disposition?

An example of such conditioning would be a little boy repeatedly throwing a ball into a pond or against a wall, which he will naturally tend to do at increasing speed. It is obvious that such an activity could inadvertently result in good training for, say, later pitching skills.

Naturally, if he happens to also aim at some particular point or object, he would also be aiding the development of accuracy, as well as power. However, as you will soon learn, these skills, as well as all other skills, are best mastered separately before they are combined. In fact, the sooner they are combined in their development, the lesser the potential.

Imagine how the training enjoyment would be enhanced if by hitting either a vertical (directional) line or a horizontal (height) line, a sensor was triggered to activate either an audio or a visual signal.

As is true of all areas of activity, the real problem is not our ignorance per se, but denial, which is the ultimate sin, because failure to face a problem precludes its resolution.

The mysterious differentiating quality in talent is not mostly in the realm of genetics, but rather, it is due to conditioning—or more specifically, methodology or approach. We are practising or training wrongly. It is not, as the old adage declares, practice which makes perfect, but practice of the right thing, which in this context means that we have been practising a skill in its entirety rather than separating it into its component parts. By practising and mastering each part individually before integrating it with the other components, our potential is determined by how well we master the individual components before their integration. Otherwise, our concentration is divided, which precludes the ultimate development of our potential.

Have we not all had that frustrating experience of trying to concentrate on something while being distracted? One of the reasons for us failing to do what is natural and obvious in these circumstances—to concentrate on one thing at a time—is our anxiousness for instant recognition and its rewards, or, put simply, greed. It is a legacy of our time.

As is often the case, the shortcut turns out, in the long run, to be not only the least economical way but also the least enjoyable way. By the same token, the natural way also turns out, in the end, to be the most fulfilling and enjoyable way. Our greed blinds us to the reality that nature, in its wisdom, has coupled its goals with enjoyment and a sense of fulfilment.

Failure to follow this approach of concentrating on one thing does not necessarily mean that you won't hit home runs, for instance, but only that, everything else being equal, you won't be as consistent. *Champion* is a relative term, not an absolute term, in that no matter how wrong our methodology is, some players will always be better than others and will rise to the top.

For instance, not being able to properly track an incoming or passing ball with the eyes forces the player to develop and rely on less-effective compensating skills, such as judgement.

To help understand how important methodology is, let's make an analogy to verbal expression. For instance, if you are not happy with the quality of your communication skills, either verbal or written, you may choose the indirect approach of reading more rather than the more direct and focused approach of recalling and interrogating the words you are using as a means of improving your ability to express yourself. Words are the building blocks of expression. The distraction of having to search for these elusive words detracts not only from the quality of your expression but, more importantly, from your thinking.

This truth substantiates the rule about the importance of practising the right thing. All practice helps, but the quality or naturalness of that practice determines both the rate and the extent of the progress.

Practice makes permanent, not perfect. At various points during the practice of the individual components of a skill, we must choose between integrating them or bringing them to a higher level of perfection.

Integration enables participation in competition sooner but also tends to limit our ultimate potential. Being anxious or greedy to demonstrate our superiority means that sport becomes subservient or only a means to the satisfaction of our greed. Our ulterior motive in this pursuit is not fulfilment, proficiency, or enjoyment, but rather the gratification of our ego or sense of identity. Mastery becomes a means instead of an end in itself, which consequently impedes its development.

In games of skill—physical or mental—external reward is not conducive to the ultimate development of creativity or accomplishment, despite arguments to the contrary. We are just now discovering this.

Unlike getting a poor mark in one subject at school, which lowers your average, having a weakness in one component of a skill in sport will drag the level of your general performance down to the level of that component because of the close interrelationship of all other components. In other words, you are no better or stronger than your weakest link.

For example, if your grasp or catching of an incoming ball is suspect, what value would fleet-footedness—or even having wings—have in getting to it? Conversely, if you are slow in getting to the ball, what value would a safe pair of hands have?

In addition to this, it is not always clear where the weakness is, and weakness in one aspect can affect another.

For instance, from an amateur perspective, if a player fears he will drop the ball, he may be slow in responding or getting to it, either subconsciously or otherwise. His reasoning may be that a player is less likely to be ridiculed for not getting to the ball than getting to it and dropping it through clumsiness.

As concentration is so crucial or central to this approach, it warrants some special attention. We have all heard the expression 'poor powers of concentration', implying that the cause of such a sporting weakness may be psychological or even deeper in the realm of genetics and therefore even less accessible—and less alterable.

A psychological problem such as poor confidence is usually the effect or complication of a deeper cause, which can be labelled a competence deficiency, usually a result of poor methodology. The resulting failure usually leads to negative thinking, which then predisposes the individual to additional failures in a type of vicious circle. We must be careful not to put the proverbial cart before the horse.

This particular error of methodology in concentration, as in other endeavours, is skipping and advancing too quickly to the next phase of an activity before completely understanding or mastering the previous phase, on which comprehending the latter phase depends. This effectively prevents one from focusing one's undivided attention on that next or subsequent phase.

It is then only natural and healthy for the mind to break off concentration at this point as a means of preserving its sanity. The experience of repeated failure can be debilitating and can lead to psychological complications, such as impressing on the subconscious mind suggestions of stupidity, a label far less tolerable than being accused of poor effort. The inattentiveness here is basically the manifestation of a psychological defence mechanism.

The overlooking or missing of some point by the student (on which the comprehension of additional information depends), coupled with the failure or natural limitations of the system to determine just what this oversight is, conspires to undermine competence and, in turn, effort.

Winning Orientation

We are encouraged, especially these days, to not only want to win, but to win at all costs. Apart from being blatantly selfish, this is another form of distraction, keeping our full concentration away from the correct mechanics or execution of a skill, and on the outcome.

While you can affect how well you execute a task through concentration, the outcome is something not ordained to be within your control.

Concern over this can only lead to anxiety, which translates to an additional distraction. We are trying to eliminate distraction, not increase it.

If you become anxious over winning, you are at the same time inescapably wishing an opponent ill fortune. This attitude or posture is inherently selfish and therefore wrong. An opponent wishing that you will fall over and break your neck does not justify you wishing a similar fate on him. Two wrongs do not make a right. If the natural law for our happiness were selfishness, we would all be doomed.

Of more significance than any consideration of morals is the question of concentration and distraction. Nevertheless, studies do inadvertently suggest some correlation between morality and efficiency. By immorally poisoning an opposing team, it is not inconceivable that you might win the game; however, the immediate gain would hardly compensate for the greater ultimate loss to the reasoning faculties. Illogical suggestions must be implanted in the subconscious mind to rationalise the inevitable guilt—unless, of course, such destructive desensitising had already been done, thereby reinforcing those previously instilled illogical suggestions.

In the long run, your proficiency at a particular skill, such as kicking or catching a ball, is determined by how well you have mastered the individual component parts of that skill. While you may improve your performance by practising the particular skill in its entirety, the most efficient approach is to divide and conquer.

All this would seem to support an old religious proverb which says that in giving up, you shall receive. We can alter the interpretation slightly to mean that instead of giving up the mere wanting, we should give up the excessive and abnormal wanting—the wanting of more than others, or in a word, greed. This is a distraction from attainment and is therefore counterproductive. By becoming more mechanics- or performance-orientated and less reward-orientated, you are moving away from both distraction and selfishness. If you feel your standard of play is unacceptable, you have two logical options: either play less-talented opposition or return to the drawing board, devoting more time to the correct practice—that of the basics. The most efficient way to raise your performance is to practise and improve the individual components of a skill, especially the weaker components, rather than practising the integrated or composite skill.

The primary focus, especially in the early grades of sport, should not be on winning, but on improving. There are countless unreliable ways of cutting corners or winning via means other than skill alone. For instance, if only winning counted, you might accomplish this through such peripheral means as playing unduly hard (and risking injury); cheating, dishonesty, or playing dirty; playing less-talented sides (and inhibiting advancement); giving most of the play to a few of the better players, thereby depriving the less skilful players of participation and improvement; or bribery and blackmail.

It's not as if the human race has never understood the connection between practising the basics and achieving results. The old masters certainly did. We probably cannot argue that they were less greedy, but they certainly inhabited a far different, slower-paced, and more naive world, far more conducive to the patience needed to practise the basics. Harking back to my analogy of words as the building blocks of expression, this is the equivalent of improving expression through mastery of words. The old masters were able to concentrate on the building blocks underlying the potential for their creations to endure for centuries. How long will ours endure?

SPORTS APPLICATIONS

A broad range of representative sports has been selected and presented in the following pages to demonstrate the benefits of putting these principles to the test.

BASKETBALL

Shooting for a basket in basketball is mostly about getting the distance and direction right. The latter factor is labelled a key component, meaning that you need only to practise that particular component of the skill to master the whole skill. In this sport, presuming that your methodology or approach is correct, a distance problem could be attributed to, say, an eye defect. This means that if your practising average at a certain distance (that is, the measure of your ability to shoot straight) is 85 per cent, for instance, and your average for actually sinking baskets is not commensurate, say, 65 per cent (which allows for a normal distance error of 20 per cent), there must be another problem, such as a depth perception error attributable to an eye defect.

Traditionally, when an athlete executes any skill, such as taking a shot at a basket, his attention is always divided between the mechanics of the shot and the outcome—in other words, the means and the end. It is this ratio that mostly differentiates the amateur from the professional. The amateur is more goal-orientated and consequently less mechanics-orientated. A slump means that a professional's focus has shifted more from the mechanics to the outcome through his increasing anxiety over mounting failure. In fact, a slump demonstrates the effect of the focus shifting from execution to outcome. An amateur, in a sense, can be described as someone in a permanent slump.

It is only when the professional regains concentration on his technique and gets his mind off outcomes that grow more mind-bending with each successive failure that he is able to move on. The increasing anxiety translates to physical tension and 'cramping up', which adversely affects the performance. This in turn compounds the increasing anxiety in a vicious cycle. The mounting anxiety of desperately wanting to score and break the slump increasingly draws the attention away from the best means of achieving that objective, which is through concentrating on the basics or the technique. The subsequent failure flowing from the anxiety will then reinforce the anxiety ad infinitum. He has unwittingly manoeuvred himself into a trap or a catch-22 situation.

It is almost impossible to condition your thinking away from results and on to basics during an important game, where anxiety is much higher than normal. If you attempted to do so at that crucial time, you would only be kidding yourself. Such reorientation efforts must first be introduced during practice, from where the benefits will gradually filter through to the contest.

As indicated, people advance at various rates in training because of their ratio—that is, according to what percentage of their focus *happens* to be on the correct mechanics, and what percentage is on other extraneous things, like results or rewards (or even, dare I say, on such techniques or modern innovations as visualisation and positive thinking).

The word *happens* is purposely emphasised because correct focus has usually been more fortuitous or accidental than deliberate, or has not really resulted from any true understanding of the underlying principles. Also, while we all claim that we have been concentrating on the basics, we have really only been paying that rule lip service.

To demonstrate, let's take a simple thing like keeping our eyes on a ball as an incoming object. How do we know how well this has been achieved? You would think that for such an important facet of so many sports, we would have some objective means of measurement. We cannot correctly judge by results, because we can achieve them by other compensating means, such as judgement.

Despite having no scientific or objective means of measurement, we can safely assume that some players perform better at this skill of tracking than others. Since normal eye movement variation in early life is only slight, we now know that this ability is more likely related to conditioning through some unrelated activity. This tracking skill, like all other skills, can be developed with the proper approach to training.

... EARLY TRACKING ...

To help understand how this can be done, consider a fan (not the sports type) whose fast-whirling blades are just a blur to the vision of the average uninitiated person, similar to the way an incoming baseball, cricket ball, or tennis ball is indistinct to the average athlete.

With perseverance, you can train your eyes to follow the spinning blade of a fan, even to the extent, if you wish, of eventually being able to read a message written on it. This means that to highly trained eyes, the blades will appear to have almost stopped. The more closely and evenly the eye movement duplicates or simulates the blade movement, the slower the blades appear to be travelling. It is similar with an incoming object, the movement type of which, incidentally, is a more natural one to the eyes than a rotating movement.

The slower an object moves—or in this case, seems to move—the better you can see it. And the better you can see it, the easier it is to hit or make contact with. In order to eventually successfully track a rapidly moving object, you must first start at slower speeds to be able to train or condition your eye muscles to develop the necessary smooth and rapid eye movement to accommodate faster speeds.

It is the scientific way. Otherwise, it would be like a weightlifter training by trying to lift a barbell that is well beyond his capacity or weight limit. Instead of gradually conditioning and developing his muscles to accommodate gradual weight increases, he is more likely to injure or strain them in the process of neglecting the basics.

The ball, at first, must be travelling slow enough for a player to be able to get at least a glimpse of it in order to have some sort of basis on which to build, whereas seeing only a blur makes it impossible to get started or to start tracking.

This pinpoints the problem in that seldom do we normally encounter those conditions. Only the lucky few catch up, while the majority are always chasing and never get the opportunity to properly train or condition their eyes.

Can you imagine what it would be like if the ball came at you in slow motion?

If you have an accommodation or adaptation speed of, say, 20 mph (32 km/h), you can, with the proper conditioning, train your eyes to be able to track an object (that is, follow an object clearly) moving at 30 mph (48 km/h) and, of course, from there to 40 mph (65 km/h) and so on. The essential point is that without the necessary training or conditioning of the intrinsic eye muscles, they are incapable of immediately jumping from only being able to follow an object travelling at, say, 20 mph (32 km/h) to trying to follow an object moving at, say, 80 mph (130 km/h) or more, which would be more akin to the actual speed of an incoming ball or object in a game. This means that the deficient person must cast about for some inevitably less efficient compensatory skill, like judgement.

To better understand this, let's make an analogy to juggling. If you wanted to learn to juggle six pins, would you throw them all into the air at once? The argument is not that few might eventually succeed, but that it is the hard way and that even with practice and endurance, most would not succeed at anything except knocking themselves out. No one can 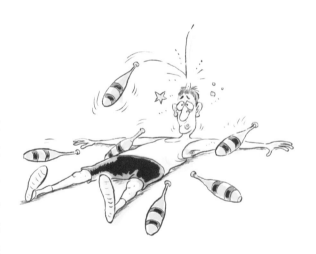 argue against the idea here that the most economical, efficient approach would be to add pins gradually as you master the technique. The gross approach only appears quicker at first. If, for instance, your life depended on juggling six pins simultaneously within one hour, then your best bet might be to throw them all up at once and hope for the best. We are doing just this to some extent when we start out by trying to hit home runs every time we step up to the plate.

The difference between the amateur and the professional is not so much that the professional is naturally quicker and more deft, but that the amateur did not advance to a greater number of pins before he first mastered the simpler task. Most so-called natural talent really results from the earlier development or practice of a related task or skill. Nevertheless, the amateur will usually find that by going back and practising more with fewer pins, his progress will be more dramatic. He had previously skipped or advanced too quickly to gain the necessary conditioning. The key is to return to the simpler activity and gradually raise it to a higher standard before undertaking a more complex task. By going fast, you go slow, and vice versa. The point is not that natural talent does not exist, but that most of the difference between athletes is the result of conditioning. Calling it natural talent is just a convenient way of hiding our ignorance. With the right training approach, natural talent can be created.

In shooting for a basket in basketball, the only component you have to practise is direction, as distance follows naturally here, unless, as mentioned, you have some eye defect. You must then rigorously apply the isolation rule and eliminate all distractions, principally the hoop or basket itself.

Some suggestions for circumventing the distraction of the basket or hoop in practice are to draw a vertical line on a wall and practise hitting it from all angles and distances; practise on a round pole that is ideally the circumference of the hoop (the deflection angle should be such that the ball will return to you if you are accurate); or my favourite, deliberately shoot short at the front rim of the hoop, and the ball deflection angle will tell you how straight the shot was.

Since you are intentionally avoiding baskets, you have effectively eliminated the distraction. Or more accurately, since the rim itself is still a target of sorts and thus a distraction, you have eliminated most of the distraction, which is the reaching out or the anxiety behind trying to hit a target, which in this case means trying to sink a basket. You can see from this that what we mean by distraction alludes less to the physical type than to the psychological type, which is usually far more disturbing. If, for instance, you can psychologically ignore the distraction of a target, such as goalposts, you can practise with them without deceiving yourself that they don't constitute a distraction.

Ideally, a vertical line used in conjunction with an audio and visual feedback, as alluded to earlier, would provide not only the means of objective judgement but also heightened enjoyment.

There is a close correlation between the success in hitting a straight vertical line and your ability to score baskets. If you are not satisfied with your scoring average, then the best way to improve that average is to return to the basics. Practise more at trying to shoot straight rather than trying to sink baskets, which, of course, is the sublime objective.

Understanding this will help eliminate frustration, which itself detracts from performance, because now you will know just what you have to do to improve your accuracy. With practice and perseverance, you will learn to think like a new breed of basketball player who no longer thinks in terms of scoring but who will now judge his performance strictly by how straight the shot was, knowing full well that his scoring percentage is intimately related to how straight he shoots. It is a law as immutable as the law of gravity. It is possible, of course, to score a basket despite a directional error, because aside from the agency of the backboard, a basketball can manage to slide on the side of the hoop if the distance component of the shot happens to be precise—a fact which any seasoned player understands.

Of course, again, it is obvious why people are reaching out for results. It is another form of greed for recognition and its rewards, a violation of the natural law which will ultimately cause only failure and unhappiness. After all, sport enjoys no immunity in that, for most of us, it is essentially just another means to a selfish end. Competence, which comes mostly through conditioning, leads to relaxation and natural confidence, which in turn enhances competence. We mustn't mistake the symptom (confidence) for the cause (competence).

Changing your orientation is not often easy, especially after years of being told by society to think a certain way, but the inevitable improvement in your ability to sink baskets will reassure you of the correctness of this approach, which, rest assured, will happen to the degree that you can get your mind off baskets.

Another important facet of this game, as it is of some others, is ball disposal, the quality of which depends on one's ability to keep track of the other players. The isolation rule here means you must practise this skill by itself and not while participating in a game where there are too many distractions to concentrate.

One method of accomplishing this might be to, as a spectator, single out one particular player to follow in a game, in addition to following the game itself. As you become adept at this, keep adding other players to follow around, being cautious not to proceed too fast before you are proficient at this, because, as mentioned, your potential—which in this instance ultimately means the quality of your disposal—is determined by how well you master the component parts of the skill before they are integrated. It should be easy to see how much easier disposal becomes the more clearly you can see more players in the game.

Using your ingenuity, you may also practise player tracking in relation to other situations, such as with the balls on a pool table.

A characteristic of junior players especially is that they usually only see clearly the player next to them. The better the opposing players can read a player's disposal intentions, the more pressure they will apply on him, because they realise that this limitation represents their best opportunity to force errors, compounding the poor player's plight by adding pressure to deficiency. It is little wonder this type of player performs so poorly. Ironically, some may even get the often correct impression that they are being persecuted in these circumstances.

TENPIN BOWLING

Applying the 'divide and conquer' principle to tenpin bowling means again eliminating as many distractions as possible, including the pins, in an effort to develop consistency, as demonstrated by consistent delivery.

Being a simple action, there are no other components in bowling to worry about apart from the delivery, which really means that the key is to develop consistency by duplicating the action each time, much like a robot. As in any unvarying or routine activity, where the same basic movement is required for every shot, developing consistency is synonymous with developing accuracy. This means that if you miss a target, you will miss it each time by exactly the same margin of error. This then requires only a fine adjustment of the position or angle of the player relative to the target—in this instance, the pins—to rectify the situation. When you reach the stage where there is a need for only fine-tuning, you are almost there.

The application of this principle, quite logically, would have led to what is now called spot bowling, whereby innovation, although pre-empting this information, is nevertheless a substantiation of those principles.

Either bowlers are brighter than their counterparts in other sports, or the need for such a natural refinement or improvement was more obvious in their discipline. Nevertheless, they ingeniously took the first step in the right direction, if not by completely eliminating the distraction of the pins, then at least by partially eliminating them by focusing on a closer, more neutral object—the markings at the beginning of the alley.

Most bowlers have found this method to be superior to watching the pins themselves, which are not going anywhere. The closer a target is, the easier it is to hit. Most bowlers discover that there is a close correlation between their ability to hit such a mark and their accuracy in knocking down the pins.

With all the emphasis on consistency, the pins are not only not useful but also cause a distraction. For instance, a strike does not necessarily tell you that you executed the basics properly. In bowling, this is achieved mostly through uniform delivery, on which the quality of your performance depends. A properly executed shot means that each shot is identical to the next. It is as simple as that.

So all that now remains for a bowler to do is to completely eliminate the distraction—the pins. You will find that your consistency will be proportionate to your success in achieving this during practice.

This is not just meant to involve a few practice shots without the pins before a game, which is the custom anyway, but rather to completely reverse your approach so that 95 per cent of all your bowling is without the pins—that is, if you are serious about your progress. Oddly enough, if you had access to an alley, you would discover that until you became proficient (which here means consistent), such an approach in itself can also be quite fulfilling and enjoyable. It is part of a natural evolution, like learning to crawl before you start to walk. Does a baby look disappointed because he or she cannot walk until he or she is about ready? Even developing into a 'mechanical' man or woman (no matter how unnatural such an objective or aspiration may seem to be) is, oddly enough, in itself fulfilling. In other more complicated sports or activities, perfection of the individual component skills almost spontaneously leads to their interaction.

FOOTBALL

The art of kicking a football involves separate skills, such as accuracy, placement of the ball on the foot, power, and so on. This activity is another example of one in which there is a key component. All we need to concentrate on here is how squarely the ball is placed on the foot and, as the expression goes, 'everything else will follow'.

However, again we must take extreme care to isolate that component from every other component and distraction, which includes removing anything that may act as a target, such as a person or goalposts, for example. Otherwise, some of the focus or concentration will be on accuracy and not where it should be, which is 100 per cent on placement or foot–ball contact. The accuracy of the kick depends on the accuracy of the placement.

Typically, after instructing his son on the fundamentals of punting, a father will have the child face the target, be it either himself or the goalposts. This will unwittingly introduce a distraction to the son's concentration on placement, which, however surprising it may sound, will have the nett effect of retarding his progress.

If the child hits the target, the father praises him, wrongly presuming that this confirms the notion that the technique must be correct. Logically, it doesn't, as it is quite possible to get a favourable result without executing the basics properly. The father might even ask, which is more important—technique or results? He would be right if the 'fault' that contributed to the success was a consistent one, which, as occasionally happens, could assure the same good result repeatedly, leading observers to describe such a technique or player as unorthodox. The point is, there are many methods of doing something the wrong way, which implies inconsistency, but there is usually only one method of doing it the right way, which means consistency. It is much easier to move from consistency to accuracy. Give me consistency, and I will promise you accuracy.

To further illustrate this point, consider a football-kicking machine, which is calibrated to administer a measured, consistent force to the football placed on a carriage in front of it. By shifting the ball just a few millimetres off-centre, you will alter considerably, where the ball lands, demonstrating the importance of accurate placement. You should practise this skill until you are able to consistently place the ball squarely, at will, on the exact centre of your foot, before introducing any other components, such as accuracy through targets or power, which have the potential to cause distraction.

The connection between precise placement of the ball on the foot and accuracy or control should now be obvious. The direction of the trajectory is altered simply by effecting a change in body position relative to the target. It is not before becoming adept at this basic skill that a player should try to influence direction through another agency, such as trying to kick off the side of the boot. In having more than one variable, he will be confused about the source of any error, knowledge of which is a prerequisite to its elimination. This is the main reason players seem to go back and forth trying to correct annoying faults.

Proper foot placement here requires the diligent removal of all targets. There are several ways of initially accomplishing this, such as kicking into the sun or using a cap drawn down to just above the eyes to prevent one from seeing where the ball goes. If your progress is not rapid, you can assume that you have overlooked something which is acting as a target, because when it is done correctly, the improvement in your kicking will be phenomenal.

You add or integrate power only after the mastery of placement. The greater the power, the lesser the accuracy. Some players will argue that this rule is not correct, claiming that the harder they kick, the more accurate they are, perhaps overlooking other extenuating factors such as having had more practice at kicking harder, or even nervousness.

The development of skills involved in catching an object, such as a ball, is as paramount in football as in most other ball sports. Separating this skill into its various components highlights a conglomeration of myriad talents, such as judgement of trajectory (incorporating both the direction and distance of the ball), reflex and speed of the start or movement of the player towards the ball, running speed, ability to track the ball with the eyes, jumping, balance, grasp, agility, coordination, and timing. With all this in place, your ability to make contact with the ball at the highest point of your leap would be advantageous in a contested catch situation. Again, applying the rule, all should be practised in isolation and gradually integrated as they are mastered. However, it is not as complicated as it may initially appear. This skill happens to have the most components of any skill.

A common characteristic of an amateur player is the hesitation he might display in pursuit of an object. This wasting of precious milliseconds often means the difference between getting or not getting to the ball. Of course, as already illustrated, there can be hidden psychological factors involved, wherein such a player, being less than confident about catching the object, may deliberately get there late, as it is less intolerable not to have reached the ball than to have reached it and dropped it.

One way to practise this is to have someone kick to the different points of a compass, with the runner concentrating only on reaching the ball, which initially means deliberately not catching it, as that will act as a distraction to getting there with the maximum potential speed. In practising this component, you should only either slap the ball down or tap it lightly. This way, your reflex and speed will improve, and you will surprise yourself with a new-found ability to get to balls which you previously would have considered beyond your reach (when you were also trying to catch them).

Catching is introduced or integrated only after you have reached your maximum speed; otherwise, once you integrate it with another component, additional progress will be impeded or will become less efficient.

The rule dictates that to the extent that you have not mastered a component, you will be distracted by it during the execution of the shot or play. This lessens concentration, which, of course, underlies proficiency.

Another component of running after and catching an object is catching it with your arms fully extended when required, like when the effort to catch is contested; otherwise, the safest catch would be on your chest.

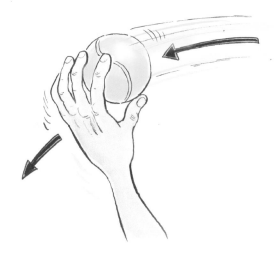

To consistently catch at the end or the highest point of your reach, you must apply the rule and practise this timing art by itself, separate from any other skill or form of distraction. This may best be achieved first by just tossing the ball a short distance into the air and increasing the distance gradually as you master the timing of touching (not catching) it at the very end of your outstretched hands. This can become a challenge and a game in its own right.

You will notice that you will gradually develop the knack of timing your leap so that your hands meet the ball at the highest point of your extended body and arms to maximise your advantage over an opponent.

To perfect the art of grasping the ball, you must time it so that you commence the backward movement or recoil of your hands at the precise moment the ball reaches them. The better they follow or track the ball, the slower the ball will seem to be travelling. The slower an object moves—or in this case, seems to move—the easier it is to catch. The key here is the tracking, whether it be catching a ball, as illustrated here, or hitting an object or ball, such as in cricket or baseball. Ultimately, it will almost seem like you are plucking a suspended object, such as a ball, out of the air. Again, this exercise should be practised in isolation and not while jumping or running after the ball.

If you practise this correctly, you will become quite confident in an area which is a common source of anxiety to many players, especially at the amateur level, because their greatest dread is dropping the ball. Again, theoretically, if the backward movement of your hands or the recoil exactly matches the speed of the incoming object, it will be equivalent to grasping a stationary object or one suspended in mid-air, which should be within everyone's ability or grasp.

GOLF

The Swing

Since, as the expression goes, 'it is all in the swing', we don't have to bother ourselves too much about the other components of the golf approach, such as power and accuracy, as they follow quite naturally.

Applying the isolation principle here means, amongst other things, that we cannot initially use a golf ball in practice, as it will constitute too much of a distraction to concentrate on the swing. The more ingrained and consistent the practice swing before the introduction of the ball is, the less vulnerable its duplication will be to such a distraction.

By *consistent*, here we mean that each swing is identical to every other and that there is little or no variation in the path of the club, especially as it passes through the tee or ball contact area.

Naturally, some objective means of measurement would be ideal here, as it would be incidental in some other instances. However, not yet having this, we must rely on our own judgement, which will improve with the recognition and acceptance of the player that there is usually too much variation in the practice swing, despite appearances or impressions. Therefore, the consistency of your practice swing determines the consistency of your game swing, which mostly determines what your handicap will be. We must shift our focus away from the more anxiety-laden ball to the less-charged swing itself, in line with the great principle 'In giving up something, you shall receive'.

A few millimetres' variation in the club–ball contact will—again, through the multiplier effect—result in an increasing magnitude of error the further the ball goes down the fairway.

Beyond achieving a mechanical uniform swing once the ball is introduced, we have the problem of not allowing it to affect that swing. Naturally, as previously illustrated, the more ingrained or established the swing is, the less likely it is to be affected by the distraction of the ball. Most players will still have to take additional precautions to ensure against this and the consequent inconsistency.

Despite having practised without a ball, actually just seeing the ball initially makes it difficult—if not impossible—to ignore, causing it to become an almost insurmountable obstacle and distraction to the swing. Somehow, we must first remove the ball from our view or at least our mind. This in itself will present a challenge to our ingenuity.

Perhaps using special spectacles or disguising the ball by putting it amongst bogus balls so the golfer doesn't know when he is about to hit the real one may prove of some help to some athletes. We are just playing here with suggestions that are neither infallible nor terribly ingenious for that matter. We are limited only by our imagination, and I am sure others will come up with better applications of the principle.

In most cases, the removal of the ball is the only certain way of getting it out of your mind. The ideal is, if possible, to gradually introduce the ball no faster than the mind can tolerate it.

The third phase of the concentration principle here is that when the golfer is ready to introduce the ball, he must initially also be prevented or insulated from knowing where the ball went. That kind of feedback can also constitute a distraction to the perfection of the shot or swing. In addition, you cannot always judge by results. You can, however, achieve them through compensation, although as also previously illustrated, there is nothing sacrosanct about executing the prescribed swing if your own unorthodox swing is consistent.

Feedback is vital, of course, but the feel of the impact of the club head on the ball will usually tell you how well or squarely you have hit it.

If you doubt the distraction that the ball has on the player, consider the difference between the average player's practice swing and his game swing. In practice, it is often difficult to distinguish the good amateur or semi-professional golfer from the professional. When we put that ball down, it is usually the death sentence, as we tend to cramp up when eye meets ball, even if imperceptibly.

As mentioned, the amateur is not 'grooving' or 'channelling' his practice swing either because he does not fully appreciate its importance or is misleading himself in the absence of any scientific or objective means of measurement. Of course, not having accomplished this without the added distraction of the target or ball just about makes it impossible to ever accomplish it—especially once the dreaded ball is introduced.

When professional golf instructors and training manuals advise us to visualise or indulge in autosuggestion and positive thinking as we hit the ball, they are unintentionally misguiding us. It may sound like good advice on the surface, but in essence, it is actually just another form of distraction from concentration on the mechanics or basics; it is counterproductive. In human affairs, when we lack the truth or the correct methodology, we tend to become more interested in the monetary potential rather than in finding the truth. We exploit the void.

Anything that may cause a distraction to our concentration on the basics—including suggestions, both negative and positive—is wrong. It is not the type of suggestion but the suggesting itself that is at fault. This does not allude to the cultivation of a positive outlook in one's life, but to the subliminal positive conditioning of the subconscious mind, causing distraction and robbing our conscious mind of control, regardless of how laudable the objective is. It is an example of the tail wagging the dog. We are compromising sovereignty for trivial objectives. At the execution stage, we should not be indulging even in positive thinking, which is a distraction to 100 per cent of the concentration on the proper execution of the swing. Allow nothing, either extrinsic or intrinsic, to distract you. Once you fully realise the true value of this type of concentration, you will find that you have no need for hocus-pocus.

You will have to condition yourself to accept that it is preferable to have a good consistent swing than an occasional good hit, because hitting the ball consistently well depends on a consistent swing. You want to be a good swinger, not a good hitter. Being a good swinger ensures you are becoming a good hitter. Concentrate on the means, and the end will follow.

The Putt

Putting in golf basically comprises two components: distance and direction. Again, in accordance with these principles, they must be practised separately or in isolation, which, of course, initially means without the use of the hole. Such a target encompasses both distance and direction, creating a distraction to the practice and development of either one individually.

You practise distance by seeing how close you can come to a horizontal line; you practise direction by seeing how close you can come to a vertical line or perhaps to the principal axis of the hole itself. Providing that you either cover up the hole or deliberately shoot past it, you will reduce its power to act as a target—and thus a distraction. It may seem to be a somewhat unexciting approach, but as illustrated elsewhere, what is natural does tend to also contain some enjoyment and fulfilment if psychological barriers are not erected. Despite whatever preconceived notions may exist or whatever arguments there may be to the contrary, there is no more efficient way.

Of course, if your direction is dead straight and the speed of the ball is not too great, it will often pop up into the air when it hits the rim of the hole and sometimes land in it. As an aside to this, in order to putt well on uneven surfaces, one must first master the simpler task of putting well on even surfaces.

If you were able to crawl behind the mind of the professional, you would discover that, unlike the amateur, who hopes the result is favourable, the professional tends to take a favourable result for granted if he is satisfied that his swing was correct. It is almost as if the two conditions are synonymous.

He is either unable or unwilling to explain to the amateur how confidence enters the equation. He is confident that if his swing is correct, he will hit the ball well—not that if he is confident, he will hit the ball well. It is a subtle but crucial difference.

If the approach or methodology is wrong, all the confidence in the world will not change things. At best, it will only help you be the best amongst those who are wrong. Confidence quite naturally follows competence. It is the experience of the intimate relationship between execution and result that leads the professional to the expectation of success or confidence. Positive orientation, in turn, is most conducive to the development of competence. All this is open to misinterpretation, not only by the casual observer but also by the golfer. Think of confidence as being *conducive* to the development of competence, not as a *substitute* for it.

Improvement in any average golfer—one who has at least an understanding of how to swing a club properly—will depend, more than anything else, on how well he succeeds at getting his mind off the ball on contact and in flight. When you are concentrating on the mechanics, it is a physical and therefore emotionally neutral activity or pursuit, but when your focus shifts to results or outcome, it becomes an emotionally charged activity akin to greed, which can then result in distraction. As a catalyst for anxiety and conflict, greed is not only morally wrong but is also technically and strategically wrong in the context of sport or any physical or mental endeavour.

TENNIS, BASEBALL, AND CRICKET

... TAKING YOUR EYES OFF THE BALL ...

We are all repeatedly told to keep our eyes on the oncoming ball, but how can we tell if a player has succeeded at this? We have already argued that judging by results is an unreliable method, as it is usually possible through some form of compensation, such as judgement, to hit the ball well enough without having kept eyes on it. The outcome might conceivably mislead one to the erroneous assumption that the player kept an eye on the ball.

It may be illuminating to experience the difference between throwing a ball up in the air and following it with your eyes only half the way down into your hands, as opposed to following it all the way into your hands. With some practice, you will understand the advantage of the latter.

Without some objective means of measurement to indicate just how well you have succeeded at this task, progress for most will not be as dramatic.

Similar to tracking a spinning fan, you can, with proper conditioning of the eyes, learn to read the label on a rapidly revolving stereo record, which would originally appear as only a blur to untrained vision. Comparing it again to learning to see the spinning blades of a fan clearly, you must start at a speed slow enough for you to comfortably pick up the movement of the object and read it clearly, increasing the speed as the intrinsic and extrinsic eye muscles engage or develop the necessary tracking movements.

Ideally, you would have a modified tennis ball machine tossing balls past you while you do nothing else but try to pick up the codes or markings on them. This arrangement would make it possible for you to learn just how well you are tracking or seeing the passing object. Its speed should be able to be regulated to encourage gradual eye engagement.

Addressing the ball from the correct position is an important facet of playing tennis. This skill, again, is best achieved by practising it exclusively, without also endeavouring to hit the ball. This may mean practising without a tennis racquet (being careful not to give others the impression you cannot afford one).

The point is that if you combine such swinging with actually hitting the ball, some of your attention and focus will be on that objective also, thus violating the rule of isolation and concentration.

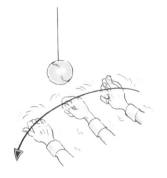

Similarly, in trying to develop topspin, isolation here may be done by suspending a ball on a string, enabling you to wholly concentrate on developing the proper wrist action. Additionally, with this approach, you will get much more practice within the same time span, better enabling you to perfect this facet of your game in line with sport's golden rule: 'The right practice makes perfect'.

BATTING

To develop consistent batting (as in baseball, for instance), you must begin by effectively bunting[1] balls (holding the bat out without swinging it), starting with balls that travel towards you no faster than your ability allows you to reasonably track them with your eyes.

You can then either gradually increase the power behind the bunt or the speed of the incoming ball as you master this facet, remembering that getting ahead of yourself by prematurely increasing swing power or ball speed ironically contains the hidden danger of retarding your potential.

By going too fast, you go too slow.

Your batting average in this regard means the percentage of times you hit the ball well or squarely, with the varying degrees of power or force used (bunting, light hitting, medium hitting, and heavy hitting).

If your bunting average is, say, 60 per cent, your light hitting average has to be less, because the more you increase the power of the swing, the more you sacrifice accuracy. Likewise, if your light hitting average (LHA) is, say, 50 per cent, your medium hitting average (MHA) has to be less again, and so on.

The most economical way to improve your LHA is to practise bunting, and the best way to improve your MHA is to practise your LHA. However, if your

---

1   The equivalent strategy in cricket would involve blocking balls.

bunting is deficient, you should go back to stage one and try to improve that average first.

If your bunting average is good or there is only little room for improvement there, you should move on to the next stage, which involves light swinging power. This 'law of gradualism' approach is natural and is thus fulfilling and enjoyable.

RIFLE SHOOTING

If you were to ask a good shot what the essence of his marksmanship was, he would probably nominate just about everything under the sun, including confidence, except for the real differentiating factor—steadiness. Perhaps his thinking is that such an attribute is not ennobling enough or is just too deep or fundamental to be altered, so why even mention it? Separating shooting into its component parts, we find such factors as steadiness, trigger squeeze, judgement of windage, breathing, and so on. Steadiness is by far the most important. Without steadiness, you should go home, as you will be too greatly handicapped; but with it, everything else will follow.

In line with the rule of divide and conquer, we must then find a method or way to develop steadiness in isolation to everything else, to maximise concentration. As is often true, a means of detection or measurement may also double as a means of development, indicating here that it can also be used as an instrument for the development of the attribute of steadiness.

You must know precisely where you're at to be able to get to where you intend to go. Not having such a gadget early on may be no great obstacle, but at a later stage, it is crucial.

Engineers have been working to develop an instrument to measure shake (movement), incorporating a seismographic device, potentiometers, and other components. This will result in a gadget with a scale, able to be attached to the barrel of a rifle for essential measurement at the fine-tuning stage. Until such a device is available, shooters will have to continue to improvise as much as possible. Any scientific means of measuring shake or movement would be enormously helpful.

This does not overlook the possibility that any unsteadiness may arise from physiological or psychological factors, or may have such an underlying cause. Neither is this intended to imply that any lack of steadiness could be an insurmountable barrier to a shooter's development as a crack shot. It only implies that it would be far easier and more consistent if improved steadiness could be facilitated.

For example, even if all humans quite naturally shook so erratically that the sight on a gun swung from one side of the target to the other, relatively speaking there would still be champions or some who are more accurate than others. The resulting standard might not even be that far off from what it presently is, due to some compensating factor, such as judgement, developed through perseverance and experience. This is not to say that any such growth or development would contradict the fact that, for most of us, doing something the proper or natural way is doing it the most efficient way.

To tackle another component of rifle shooting or marksmanship, such as windage, before you are skilled at steadiness, trigger squeeze, breathing, and so on, introduces another variable to the range of prospective causes of error.

You would not know, for instance, if it was caused by unsteadiness or windage adjustment error. In a word, it would be illogical. Again, if progress is taken seriously, then a variable such as windage must be eliminated or nullified, which unfortunately could initially mean an indoor accommodation or a tunnel of sorts until accuracy is mastered without the distraction of the unpredictability of the wind.

If a country could determine through some kind of screening who had the steadiest hands amongst its citizens and then offered training to those who scored highest in this facet, that country would undoubtedly eventually dominate this sport. Ammunition should not be expended until a certain standard of control is achieved. Its use would not only be expensive but of little value, especially during the initial stages of developing that steadiness. While you could say that using live ammo might be of some help towards developing steadiness, in light of this information it would be an extravagant approach.

CONCLUSION

In writing this book, I actually interrupted the writing of what I consider to be two other far more important books.

The ultimate nett effect of such a book as this would only be to raise the standards of play, which, being a relative thing, would not even really affect our enjoyment of a sport—not to mention its unimportance relative to man's more serious problems.

In basketball, for instance, greater proficiency might translate to reducing the circumference of the rim size—unless, of course, higher scores were preferred, in which case the argument becomes invalid, as increasing the rim size could easily achieve that goal in the same way that baseballs have been designed to travel further.

Of course, reducing the size of the basketball would have the same effect, as might some other alterations. You must ask the question, would a smaller rim increase your enjoyment? It would seem that the only real value this information would have would be for those perceptive individuals who were the first to adopt it, thus rendering its ultimate worth dubious.

One of the other two books to which I have alluded is *Total Word Recall*, which aims to teach readers how to readily recall those elusive "must" words that will help produce better communicators, and thus leaders, not just listeners, readers or followers. The other, *The Cosmic Law*, explores the key to understanding ourselves by focusing on personal issues such as health, depression, anxiety, fulfilment, contentment, happiness, tension, morality and the whole purpose of existence. This book is the result of the application of some of the principles found in *The Cosmic Law* to a particular subject to demonstrate their wide relevance or universality.

It is obvious that these other books should take some priority over recreation. However, one redeeming feature is that the natural principles contained within this book have broad application to not only those sports that it references but to all sports; not only to all sports but to all physical activities; and finally, not only to all physical activities but to all learning, both physical and mental. So perhaps the digression was at least partially justified after all. I hope you agree. Rather than arriving at the end, this may be just the beginning of your journey to fulfilment.

ABOUT THE AUTHOR

Eugene Joseph McConnin
20 October 1930–8 November 2016

A native New Yorker, Eugene McConnin was born in Brooklyn to parents of strict Irish Catholic heritage almost a year to the day after the start of the Great Depression. He was a nine-year-old Catholic primary school student living in Long Island on the outbreak of World War II.

His father, Eugene Edwin McConnin, was a hard-working employee of Citibank's New York head office, while his mother, Rose, was a loving housewife who devoted her life to the well-being of her husband and two children, Eugene Junior and John, who was a year younger than Eugene.

Both boys grew to become accomplished sportsmen, excelling in a wide range of sporting endeavours both during and after their school years. Eugene's unique approach to every discipline was characterised by his unwavering dedication to training and the practice of specific techniques developed to gain and maintain a winning edge, while his brother, better known as Jack, rose to prominence as both a talented competitor on the national tennis circuit and as a successful lawyer.

While sport dominated Eugene's early life, winning him many awards, it was during his secondary school years at Jackson Senior High that he developed parallel passions for words and mathematics. He was widely favoured to bring home the national interschool mathematics trophy for Jackson High in his senior year, only to come up against elements of a new math system that hadn't been introduced at his school that year. He didn't win, but needless to say, he took on the challenge of wreaking his revenge and mastering the new math in the blink of an eye after the contest.

As a Cold War conscript after the outbreak of the Korean War in the 1950s, Eugene became the US Army tenpin bowling champion before being posted to Fort Polk, Louisiana, to serve as private secretary to the youngest American general to command a combat division in Korea, Major General Philip De Witt Ginder. The Korean War ended just weeks before Eugene was due to be shipped out for active service. After his discharge, he was awarded a university scholarship and chose to study chiropractic medicine, becoming a graduate of the iconic Palmer College of Chiropractic. He also studied a wide range of complementary courses.

After returning to New York, where he married his first wife, Barbara, Eugene lived and worked in Buffalo and Long island. Then he decided to migrate to Australia with their then three-year-old daughter, Sharon, setting sail on a cargo ship for an eight-week journey to Brisbane. There they were greeted by one of the worst storms ever to make landfall on the east coast of their new homeland, eroding beaches and undermining buildings in its path. It set the scene for an adventurous new chapter in Eugene's life.

Driving south to Sydney before embarking on a transcontinental crossing to Western Australia, the family headed for Geraldton, a relatively large regional centre about 400 kilometres north of the state capital Perth, where Eugene bought his first house and ran a successful chiropractic clinic for the ensuing four years.

Meanwhile, opportunity beckoned in the fast-growing Western Australian capital, which was crying out for experienced chiropractic practitioners, especially those with credentials aligned with the objectives of contemporary sports medicine. This was Eugene's bailiwick for the next twenty-five years. While living and working in the coastal suburban hub of Doubleview, his personal life took some twists and turns, starting with the breakdown of his marriage and a return to several years of bachelorhood. This was followed by the start of a new romance in 1977 and eventual marriage in 1983 to his second wife, Vicki, and the subsequent arrival of his second daughter, Jessica, later the same year. His chiropractic clinic remained successful until his retirement in 1995, which was the year his second marriage ended.

This book had its genesis in the ten-year period leading up to that point.

With Eugene constantly throwing his sports skills development findings around, open for discussion, it was Vicki who convinced him to document them, put them on paper, and share them with the world.

'Eugene and l remained friends. Living totally separate lives, I became his full-time carer in his final years,' she relates. 'My promise to him was to finally publish his books.'

Eugene continued writing, working on three entirely different books during the years immediately before and after his retirement, until his death in 2016.

INDEX

Lightning Source UK Ltd.
Milton Keynes UK
UKHW051624070223
416582UK00002B/167